NIST Special Publication 800-123

Guide to General Server Security

Recommendations of the National Institute of Standards and Technology

Karen Scarfone
Wayne Jansen
Miles Tracy

COMPUTER SECURITY

Computer Security Division
Information Technology Laboratory
National Institute of Standards and Technology
Gaithersburg, MD 20899-8930

July 2008

U.S. Department of Commerce

Carlos M. Gutierrez, Secretary

National Institute of Standards and Technology

James M. Turner, Deputy Director

Reports on Computer Systems Technology

The Information Technology Laboratory (ITL) at the National Institute of Standards and Technology (NIST) promotes the U.S. economy and public welfare by providing technical leadership for the nation's measurement and standards infrastructure. ITL develops tests, test methods, reference data, proof of concept implementations, and technical analysis to advance the development and productive use of information technology. ITL's responsibilities include the development of technical, physical, administrative, and management standards and guidelines for the cost-effective security and privacy of sensitive unclassified information in Federal computer systems. This Special Publication 800-series reports on ITL's research, guidance, and outreach efforts in computer security and its collaborative activities with industry, government, and academic organizations.

Certain commercial entities, equipment, or materials may be identified in this document in order to describe an experimental procedure or concept adequately. Such identification is not intended to imply recommendation or endorsement by the National Institute of Standards and Technology, nor is it intended to imply that the entities, materials, or equipment are necessarily the best available for the purpose.

Acknowledgements

The authors, Karen Scarfone and Wayne Jansen of the National Institute of Standards and Technology (NIST) and Miles Tracy of Federal Reserve Information Technology, wish to thank their colleagues who reviewed drafts of this document and contributed to its technical content. The authors would like to acknowledge Murugiah Souppaya, Tim Grance, and Jim St. Pierre of NIST, Robert Dutton of Booz Allen Hamilton, and Kurt Dillard for their keen and insightful assistance throughout the development of the document. Special thanks also go to the security experts that provided feedback during the public comment period, particularly Dean Farrington (Wells Fargo), Joseph Klein (Command Information), Dr. Daniel Woodard (The Bionetics Corporation), and representatives from the Federal Aviation Administration.

Much of the content of this publication was derived from NIST Special Publication 800-44 Version 2, *Guidelines on Securing Public Web Servers*, by Miles Tracy, Wayne Jansen, Karen Scarfone, and Theodore Winograd, and NIST Special Publication 800-45 Version 2, *Guidelines on Electronic Mail Security*, by Miles Tracy, Wayne Jansen, Karen Scarfone, and Jason Butterfield.

Table of Contents

Executive Summary ES-1

1. Introduction 1-1
   1.1 Authority 1-1
   1.2 Purpose and Scope 1-1
   1.3 Audience 1-2
   1.4 Document Structure 1-2

2. Background 2-1
   2.1 Server Vulnerabilities, Threats, and Environments 2-1
   2.2 Security Categorization of Information and Information Systems 2-2
   2.3 Basic Server Security Steps 2-3
   2.4 Server Security Principles 2-4

3. Server Security Planning 3-1
   3.1 Installation and Deployment Planning 3-1
   3.2 Security Management Staff 3-3
       3.2.1 Chief Information Officer 3-4
       3.2.2 Information Systems Security Program Managers 3-4
       3.2.3 Information Systems Security Officers 3-4
       3.2.4 Server, Network, and Security Administrators 3-5
   3.3 Management Practices 3-5
   3.4 System Security Plan 3-6
   3.5 Human Resources Requirements 3-7

4. Securing the Server Operating System 4-1
   4.1 Patch and Upgrade Operating System 4-1
   4.2 Hardening and Securely Configuring the OS 4-2
       4.2.1 Remove or Disable Unnecessary Services, Applications, and Network Protocols 4-2
       4.2.2 Configure OS User Authentication 4-4
       4.2.3 Configure Resource Controls Appropriately 4-6
   4.3 Install and Configure Additional Security Controls 4-6
   4.4 Security Testing the Operating System 4-7

5. Securing the Server Software 5-1
   5.1 Securely Installing the Server Software 5-1
   5.2 Configuring Access Controls 5-2
   5.3 Server Resource Constraints 5-3
   5.4 Selecting and Implementing Authentication and Encryption Technologies 5-4

6. Maintaining the Security of the Server 6-1
   6.1 Logging 6-1
       6.1.1 Identifying Logging Capabilities and Requirements 6-1
       6.1.2 Reviewing and Retaining Log Files 6-2
       6.1.3 Automated Log File Analysis Tools 6-3
   6.2 Server Backup Procedures 6-4
       6.2.1 Server Data Backup Policies 6-4

		6.2.2 Server Backup Types	6-5
		6.2.3 Maintain a Test Server	6-6
	6.3	Recovering From a Security Compromise	6-6
	6.4	Security Testing Servers	6-8
		6.4.1 Vulnerability Scanning	6-9
		6.4.2 Penetration Testing	6-10
	6.5	Remotely Administering a Server	6-11

Appendices

Appendix A— Glossary A-1

Appendix B— Acronyms and Abbreviations B-1

Appendix C— Resources C-1

Executive Summary

An organization's servers provide a wide variety of services to internal and external users, and many servers also store or process sensitive information for the organization. Some of the most common types of servers are Web, email, database, infrastructure management, and file servers. This publication addresses the general security issues of typical servers.

Servers are frequently targeted by attackers because of the value of their data and services. For example, a server might contain personally identifiable information that could be used to perform identity theft. The following are examples of common security threats to servers:

- Malicious entities may exploit software bugs in the server or its underlying operating system to gain unauthorized access to the server.

- Denial of service (DoS) attacks may be directed to the server or its supporting network infrastructure, denying or hindering valid users from making use of its services.

- Sensitive information on the server may be read by unauthorized individuals or changed in an unauthorized manner.

- Sensitive information transmitted unencrypted or weakly encrypted between the server and the client may be intercepted.

- Malicious entities may gain unauthorized access to resources elsewhere in the organization's network via a successful attack on the server.

- Malicious entities may attack other entities after compromising a server. These attacks can be launched directly (e.g., from the compromised host against an external server) or indirectly (e.g., placing malicious content on the compromised server that attempts to exploit vulnerabilities in the clients of users accessing the server).

This document is intended to assist organizations in installing, configuring, and maintaining secure servers. More specifically, this document describes, in detail, the following practices to apply:

- Securing, installing, and configuring the underlying operating system

- Securing, installing, and configuring server software

- Maintaining the secure configuration through application of appropriate patches and upgrades, security testing, monitoring of logs, and backups of data and operating system files.

The following key guidelines are recommended to Federal departments and agencies for maintaining a secure server.

Organizations should carefully plan and address the security aspects of the deployment of a server.

Because it is much more difficult to address security once deployment and implementation have occurred, security should be carefully considered from the initial planning stage. Organizations are more likely to make decisions about configuring computers appropriately and consistently when they develop and use a detailed, well-designed deployment plan. Developing such a plan will support server administrators in making the inevitable tradeoff decisions between usability, performance, and risk.

Organizations often fail to consider the human resource requirements for both deployment and operational phases of the server and supporting infrastructure. Organizations should address the following points in a deployment plan:

- Types of personnel required (e.g., system and server administrators, network administrators, information systems security officers [ISSO])

- Skills and training required by assigned personnel

- Individual (i.e., level of effort required of specific personnel types) and collective staffing (i.e., overall level of effort) requirements.

Organizations should implement appropriate security management practices and controls when maintaining and operating a secure server.

Appropriate management practices are essential to operating and maintaining a secure server. Security practices entail the identification of an organization's information system assets and the development, documentation, and implementation of policies, standards, procedures, and guidelines that help to ensure the confidentiality, integrity, and availability of information system resources. To ensure the security of a server and the supporting network infrastructure, the following practices should be implemented:

- Organization-wide information system security policy

- Configuration/change control and management

- Risk assessment and management

- Standardized software configurations that satisfy the information system security policy

- Security awareness and training

- Contingency planning, continuity of operations, and disaster recovery planning

- Certification and accreditation.

Organizations should ensure that the server operating system is deployed, configured, and managed to meet the security requirements of the organization.

The first step in securing a server is securing the underlying operating system. Most commonly available servers operate on a general-purpose operating system. Many security issues can be avoided if the operating systems underlying servers are configured appropriately. Default hardware and software configurations are typically set by manufacturers to emphasize features, functions, and ease of use, at the expense of security. Because manufacturers are not aware of each organization's security needs, each server administrator must configure new servers to reflect their organization's security requirements and reconfigure them as those requirements change. Using security configuration guides or checklists can assist administrators in securing servers consistently and efficiently. Securing an operating system initially would generally include the following steps:

- Patch and upgrade the operating system

- Remove or disable unnecessary services, applications, and network protocols

- Configure operating system user authentication

- Configure resource controls
- Install and configure additional security controls, if needed
- Perform security testing of the operating system.

Organizations should ensure that the server application is deployed, configured, and managed to meet the security requirements of the organization.

In many respects, the secure installation and configuration of the server application will mirror the operating system process discussed above. The overarching principle is to install the minimal amount of services required and eliminate any known vulnerabilities through patches or upgrades. If the installation program installs any unnecessary applications, services, or scripts, they should be removed immediately after the installation process concludes. Securing the server application would generally include the following steps:

- Patch and upgrade the server application
- Remove or disable unnecessary services, applications, and sample content
- Configure server user authentication and access controls
- Configure server resource controls
- Test the security of the server application (and server content, if applicable).

Many servers also use authentication and encryption technologies to restrict who can access the server and to protect information transmitted between the server and its clients. Organizations should periodically examine the services and information accessible on the server and determine the necessary security requirements. Organizations should also be prepared to migrate their servers to stronger cryptographic technologies as weaknesses are identified in the servers' existing cryptographic technologies. For example, NIST has recommended that use of the Secure Hash Algorithm 1 (SHA-1) be phased out by 2010 in favor of SHA-224, SHA-256, and other larger, stronger hash functions. Organizations should stay aware of cryptographic requirements and plan to update their servers accordingly.

Organizations should commit to the ongoing process of maintaining the security of servers to ensure continued security.

Maintaining a secure server requires constant effort, resources, and vigilance from an organization. Securely administering a server on a daily basis is an essential aspect of server security. Maintaining the security of a server will usually involve the following actions:

- Configuring, protecting, and analyzing log files on an ongoing and frequent basis
- Backing up critical information frequently
- Establishing and following procedures for recovering from compromise
- Testing and applying patches in a timely manner
- Testing security periodically.

1. Introduction

1.1 Authority

The National Institute of Standards and Technology (NIST) developed this document in furtherance of its statutory responsibilities under the Federal Information Security Management Act (FISMA) of 2002, Public Law 107-347.

NIST is responsible for developing standards and guidelines, including minimum requirements, for providing adequate information security for all agency operations and assets; but such standards and guidelines shall not apply to national security systems. This guideline is consistent with the requirements of the Office of Management and Budget (OMB) Circular A-130, Section 8b(3), "Securing Agency Information Systems," as analyzed in A-130, Appendix IV: Analysis of Key Sections. Supplemental information is provided in A-130, Appendix III.

This guideline has been prepared for use by Federal agencies. It may be used by nongovernmental organizations on a voluntary basis and is not subject to copyright, though attribution is desired.

Nothing in this document should be taken to contradict standards and guidelines made mandatory and binding on Federal agencies by the Secretary of Commerce under statutory authority, nor should these guidelines be interpreted as altering or superseding the existing authorities of the Secretary of Commerce, Director of the OMB, or any other Federal official.

1.2 Purpose and Scope

The purpose of this document is to assist organizations in understanding the fundamental activities performed as part of securing and maintaining the security of servers that provide services over network communications as a main function. Hosts that incidentally provide one or a few services for maintenance or accessibility purposes, such as a remote access service for remote troubleshooting, are not considered servers in this document. The types of servers this publication addresses include outward-facing publicly accessible servers, such as web and email services, and a wide range of inward-facing servers. This document discusses the need to secure servers and provides recommendations for selecting, implementing, and maintaining the necessary security controls.

This document addresses common servers that use general operating systems (OS) such as Unix, Linux, and Windows. Many of the recommendations in this document may also be applicable to servers that use specialized OSs or run on proprietary appliances, but other recommendations will not be implementable or may have unintended consequences, so such servers are considered outside the scope of this document. Other types of servers outside the scope of this document are virtual servers and highly specialized servers, particularly security infrastructure devices (e.g., firewalls, intrusion detection systems), which have unusual configurations and security needs.

Other NIST documents, such as Special Publication (SP) 800-45 Version 2, *Guidelines on Electronic Mail Security* and SP 800-44 Version 2, *Guidelines on Securing Public Web Servers*, provide recommendations for particular types of servers. The recommendations in this document are intended as a foundation for other server-related documents and do not override more specific recommendations made in such documents.

1.3 Audience

This document has been created primarily for system administrators and security administrators who are responsible for the technical aspects of securing servers. The material in this document is technically oriented, and it is assumed that readers have at least a basic understanding of system and network security.

1.4 Document Structure

The remainder of this document is organized into the following major sections:

- Section 2 provides background information about servers and presents an overview of server security concerns. It also introduces the high-level steps for securing a server.

- Section 3 discusses the security planning and management for servers.

- Section 4 presents an overview of securing a server's operating system.

- Section 5 discusses the actions needed to securely install and configure server software, such as Web server software and email server software.

- Section 6 provides recommendations for maintaining the security of a server.

The document also contains appendices with supporting material:

- Appendix A contains a glossary.

- Appendix B contains a list of acronyms and abbreviations.

- Appendix C lists print and online resources that may be helpful for understanding general server security.

2. Background

A *server* is a host that provides one or more services for other hosts over a network as a primary function.[1] For example, a file server provides file sharing services so that users can access, modify, store, and delete files. Another example is a database server that provides database services for Web applications on Web servers. The Web servers, in turn, provide Web content services to users' Web browsers. There are many other types of servers, such as application, authentication, directory services, email, infrastructure management, logging, name/address resolution services (e.g., Domain Name Server [DNS]), print, and remote access.

This section provides background information on server security. It first discusses common server vulnerabilities and threats, and places them in the context of the types of environments in which servers are deployed. Next, it explains how the security needs of a server can be categorized so that the appropriate security controls can be determined. The section also gives an overview of the basic steps that are required to ensure the security of a server and explains fundamental principles of securing servers.

2.1 Server Vulnerabilities, Threats, and Environments

To secure a server, it is essential to first define the threats that must be mitigated. Knowledge of potential threats is important to understanding the reasons behind the various baseline technical security practices presented in this document. Many threats against data and resources are possible because of mistakes—either bugs in operating system and server software that create exploitable vulnerabilities, or errors made by end users and administrators. Threats may involve intentional actors (e.g., attacker who wants to access information on a server) or unintentional actors (e.g., administrator who forgets to disable user accounts of a former employee.) Threats can be local, such as a disgruntled employee, or remote, such as an attacker in another geographical area. Organizations should conduct risk assessments to identify the specific threats against their servers and determine the effectiveness of existing security controls in counteracting the threats; they then should perform risk mitigation to decide what additional measures (if any) should be implemented, as discussed in NIST Special Publication (SP) 800-30, *Risk Assessment Guide for Information Technology Systems*. Performing risk assessments and mitigation helps organizations better understand their security posture and decide how their servers should be secured.

The baseline technical security practices presented in this publication are based on commonly accepted technical security principles and practices, documented in various NIST SPs (including SP 800-14, SP 800-23, and SP 800-53) and other sources such as the Department of Defense (DoD) *Information Assurance Technical Framework*. In particular, NIST SP 800-27, *Engineering Principles for Information Technology Security (A Baseline for Achieving Security)*, contains a set of engineering principles for system security that provide a foundation upon which a more consistent and structured approach to the design, development, and implementation of IT security capabilities can be constructed.

An important element of planning the appropriate security controls for a server is understanding the threats associated with the environment in which the server is deployed.[2] The recommendations in this publication are based on the assumption that the servers are in typical enterprise environments and thus face the threats and have the security needs usually associated with such environments. Organizations

---

[1] For the purposes of this document, a host that does not provide services for other hosts as a primary function, but incidentally provides one or a few services for maintenance or accessibility purposes, is not considered a server. An example is a laptop that has a remote access service enabled so that IT support staff can remotely maintain the laptop and perform troubleshooting.

[2] Additional information on environments is available from NIST SP 800-70, *Security Configuration Checklists Program for IT Products: Guidance for Checklists Users and Developers* (http://csrc.nist.gov/publications/PubsSPs.html).

deploying servers in higher-security environments are likely to need to employ more restrictive security controls than the recommendations in this publication. For servers in legacy environments, organizations should secure them as if they were in a typical enterprise environment or a higher-security environment, as appropriate, and make the minimum possible security control alterations to facilitate legacy access.

2.2 Security Categorization of Information and Information Systems

The classic model for information security defines three objectives of security: maintaining confidentiality, integrity, and availability. *Confidentiality* refers to protecting information from being accessed by unauthorized parties. *Integrity* refers to ensuring the authenticity of information—that information is not altered, and that the source of the information is genuine. *Availability* means that information is accessible by authorized users. Each objective addresses a different aspect of providing protection for information.

Determining how strongly a system needs to be protected is based largely on the type of information that the system processes and stores. For example, a system containing medical records probably needs much stronger protection than a computer only used for viewing publicly released documents. This is not to imply that the second system does not need protection; every system needs to be protected, but the level of protection may vary based on the value of the system and its data. Federal Information Processing Standards (FIPS) Publication (PUB) 199, *Standards for Security Categorization of Federal Information and Information System* establishes criteria for determining the security category of a system.[3] FIPS PUB 199 defines three security categories—low, moderate, and high—based on the potential impact of a security breach involving a particular system:

- "The potential impact is LOW if the loss of confidentiality, integrity, or availability could be expected to have a limited adverse effect on organizational operations, organizational assets, or individuals. A limited adverse effect means that, for example, the loss of confidentiality, integrity, or availability might (i) cause a degradation in mission capability to an extent and duration that the organization is able to perform its primary functions, but the effectiveness of the functions is noticeably reduced; (ii) result in minor damage to organizational assets; (iii) result in minor financial loss; or (iv) result in minor harm to individuals.

- The potential impact is MODERATE if the loss of confidentiality, integrity, or availability could be expected to have a serious adverse effect on organizational operations, organizational assets, or individuals. A serious adverse effect means that, for example, the loss of confidentiality, integrity, or availability might (i) cause a significant degradation in mission capability to an extent and duration that the organization is able to perform its primary functions, but the effectiveness of the functions is significantly reduced; (ii) result in significant damage to organizational assets; (iii) result in significant financial loss; or (iv) result in significant harm to individuals that does not involve loss of life or serious life threatening injuries.

- The potential impact is HIGH if the loss of confidentiality, integrity, or availability could be expected to have a severe or catastrophic adverse effect on organizational operations, organizational assets, or individuals. A severe or catastrophic adverse effect means that, for example, the loss of confidentiality, integrity, or availability might (i) cause a severe degradation in or loss of mission capability to an extent and duration that the organization is not able to perform one or more of its primary functions; (ii) result in major damage to organizational assets; (iii) result in major financial loss; or (iv) result in severe or catastrophic harm to individuals involving loss of life or serious life threatening injuries."

---

[3] FIPS PUB 199 is available for download from http://csrc.nist.gov/publications/PubsFIPS.html.

Each system, including all servers that are part of the system, should be protected based on the potential impact to the system of a loss of confidentiality, integrity, or availability. Protection measures (otherwise known as *security controls*) tend to fall into two categories. First, security weaknesses in the system need to be resolved. For example, if a system has a known vulnerability that attackers could exploit, the system should be patched so that the vulnerability is removed or mitigated. Second, the system should offer only the required functionality to each authorized user, so that no one can use functions that are not necessary. This principle is known as *least privilege*. Limiting functionality and resolving security weaknesses have a common goal: give attackers as few opportunities as possible to breach a system.

A common problem with security controls is that they often make systems less convenient or more difficult to use. When usability is an issue, many users will attempt to circumvent security controls; for example, if passwords must be long and complex, users may write them down. Balancing security, functionality, and usability is often a challenge. This guide attempts to strike a proper balance and make recommendations that provide a reasonably secure solution while offering the functionality and usability that users require.

Another fundamental principle endorsed by this guide is using multiple layers of security—defense in depth. For example, a system may be protected from external attack by several controls, including a network-based firewall, a host-based firewall, and OS patching. The motivation for having multiple layers is that if one layer fails or otherwise cannot counteract a certain threat, other layers might prevent the threat from successfully breaching the system. A combination of network-based and host-based controls is generally most effective at providing consistent protection for systems.

NIST SP 800-53 Revision 2, *Recommended Security Controls for Federal Information Systems*, proposes minimum baseline management, operational, and technical security controls for information systems.[4] These controls are to be implemented based on the security categorizations proposed by FIPS 199, as described earlier in this section. This guidance should assist agencies in meeting baseline requirements for servers deployed in their environments.

2.3 Basic Server Security Steps

A number of steps are required to ensure the security of any server. As a prerequisite for taking any step, however, it is essential that the organization have a security policy in place. Taking the following steps for server security within the context of the organization's security policy should prove effective:

1. Plan the installation and deployment of the operating system (OS) and other components for the server. Section 3 addresses this step.

2. Install, configure, and secure the underlying OS. This is discussed in Section 4.

3. Install, configure, and secure the server software. Section 5 describes this step.

4. For servers that host content, such as Web servers (Web pages), database servers (databases), and directory servers (directories), ensure that the content is properly secured. This is highly dependent on the type of server and the type of content, so it is outside the scope of this publication to provide recommendations for content security. Readers should consult relevant NIST publications (see Appendix C) and other sources of security recommendations for information on securing server content.

---

[4] NIST SP 800-53 Revision 2, created in response to FISMA, is available at http://csrc.nist.gov/publications/PubsSPs.html.

5. Employ appropriate network protection mechanisms (e.g., firewall, packet filtering router, and proxy). Choosing the mechanisms for a particular situation depends on several factors, including the location of the server's clients (e.g., Internet, internal, internal and remote access), the location of the server on the network, the types of services offered by the server, and the types of threats against the server. Accordingly, this publication does not present recommendations for selecting network protection mechanisms. NIST SP 800-41, *Guidelines on Firewalls and Firewall Policy* and NIST SP 800-94, *Guide to Intrusion Detection and Prevention Systems (IDPS)*, contain additional information on network protection mechanisms.

6. Employ secure administration and maintenance processes, including application of patches and upgrades, monitoring of logs, backups of data and OS, and periodic security testing. This step is described in Section 6.

The practices recommended in this document are designed to help mitigate the risks associated with servers. They build on and assume the implementation of practices described in the NIST publications on system and network security listed in Appendix C.

2.4 Server Security Principles

When addressing server security issues, it is an excellent idea to keep in mind the following general information security principles:[5]

- **Simplicity**—Security mechanisms (and information systems in general) should be as simple as possible. Complexity is at the root of many security issues.

- **Fail-Safe**—If a failure occurs, the system should fail in a secure manner, i.e., security controls and settings remain in effect and are enforced. It is usually better to lose functionality rather than security.

- **Complete Mediation**—Rather than providing direct access to information, mediators that enforce access policy should be employed. Common examples of mediators include file system permissions, proxies, firewalls, and mail gateways.

- **Open Design**—System security should not depend on the secrecy of the implementation or its components.

- **Separation of Privilege**—Functions, to the degree possible, should be separate and provide as much granularity as possible. The concept can apply to both systems and operators and users. In the case of systems, functions such as read, edit, write, and execute should be separate. In the case of system operators and users, roles should be as separate as possible. For example, if resources allow, the role of system administrator should be separate from that of the database administrator.

- **Least Privilege**—This principle dictates that each task, process, or user is granted the minimum rights required to perform its job. By applying this principle consistently, if a task, process, or user is compromised, the scope of damage is constrained to the limited resources available to the compromised entity.

---

[5] Derived from Matt Curtin, *Developing Trust: Online Privacy and Security*, November 2001 and from Jerome H. Saltzer and Michael Schroeder, "The Protection of Information in Computer Systems," *Proceedings of the IEEE*, Vol. 63, pages 1278–1308

- **Psychological Acceptability**—Users should understand the necessity of security. This can be provided through training and education. In addition, the security mechanisms in place should present users with sensible options that give them the usability they require on a daily basis. If users find the security mechanisms too cumbersome, they may devise ways to work around or compromise them. The objective is not to weaken security so it is understandable and acceptable, but to train and educate users and to design security mechanisms and policies that are usable and effective.

- **Least Common Mechanism**—When providing a feature for the system, it is best to have a single process or service gain some function without granting that same function to other parts of the system. The ability for the Web server process to access a back-end database, for instance, should not also enable other applications on the system to access the back-end database.

- **Defense-in-Depth**—Organizations should understand that a single security mechanism is generally insufficient. Security mechanisms (defenses) need to be layered so that compromise of a single security mechanism is insufficient to compromise a host or network. No "silver bullet" exists for information system security.

- **Work Factor**—Organizations should understand what it would take to break the system or network's security features. The amount of work necessary for an attacker to break the system or network should exceed the value that the attacker would gain from a successful compromise.

- **Compromise Recording**—Records and logs should be maintained so that if a compromise does occur, evidence of the attack is available to the organization. This information can assist in securing the network and host after the compromise and aid in identifying the methods and exploits used by the attacker. This information can be used to better secure the host or network in the future. In addition, these records and logs can assist organizations in identifying and prosecuting attackers.

3. Server Security Planning

The most critical aspect of deploying a secure server is careful planning before installation, configuration, and deployment. Careful planning will ensure that the server is as secure as possible and in compliance with all relevant organizational policies. Many server security and performance problems can be traced to a lack of planning or management controls. The importance of management controls cannot be overstated. In many organizations, the IT support structure is highly fragmented. This fragmentation leads to inconsistencies, and these inconsistencies can lead to security vulnerabilities and other issues.

3.1 Installation and Deployment Planning

Security should be considered from the initial planning stage at the beginning of the systems development life cycle to maximize security and minimize costs. It is much more difficult and expensive to address security after deployment and implementation. Organizations are more likely to make decisions about configuring hosts appropriately and consistently if they begin by developing and using a detailed, well-designed deployment plan. Developing such a plan enables organizations to make informed tradeoff decisions between usability and performance, and risk. A deployment plan allows organizations to maintain secure configurations and aids in identifying security vulnerabilities, which often manifest themselves as deviations from the plan.

In the planning stages of a server, the following items should be considered:[6]

- Identify the purpose(s) of the server.

    - What information categories will be stored on the server?

    - What information categories will be processed on or transmitted through the server?

    - What are the security requirements for this information?

    - Will any information be retrieved from or stored on another host (e.g., database server, directory server, Web server, Network Attached Storage (NAS) server, Storage Area Network (SAN) server)?

    - What are the security requirements for any other hosts involved?

    - What other service(s) will be provided by the server (in general, dedicating the host to only one service is the most secure option)?

    - What are the security requirements for these additional services?

    - What are the requirements for continuity of services provided by the server, such as those specified in continuity of operations plans and disaster recovery plans?

    - Where on the network will the server be located?

- Identify the network services that will be provided on the server, such as Hypertext Transfer Protocol (HTTP), File Transfer Protocol (FTP), Simple Mail Transfer Protocol (SMTP), Network File System

---

[6] Content derived from Julia Allen et al., *Securing Network Servers*, April 2000, http://www.sei.cmu.edu/pub/documents/sims/pdf/sim010.pdf

(NFS), or database services (e.g., Open Database Connectivity [ODBC]). The network protocols to be used for each service (e.g., IPv4, IPv6) should also be identified.

- Identify any network service software, both client and server, to be installed on the server and any other support servers.

- Identify the users or categories of users of the server and any support hosts.

- Determine the privileges that each category of user will have on the server and support hosts.

- Determine how the server will be managed (e.g., locally, remotely from the internal network, remotely from external networks).

- Decide if and how users will be authenticated and how authentication data will be protected.

- Determine how appropriate access to information resources will be enforced.

- Determine which server applications meet the organization's requirements. Consider servers that may offer greater security, albeit with less functionality in some instances. Some issues to consider include—

    - Cost

    - Compatibility with existing infrastructure

    - Knowledge of existing employees

    - Existing manufacturer relationship

    - Past vulnerability history

    - Functionality.

- Work closely with manufacturer(s) in the planning stage.

The choice of server application may determine the choice of OS. However, to the degree possible, server administrators should choose an OS that provides the following:[7]

- Ability to granularly restrict administrative or root level activities to authorized users only

- Ability to granularly control access to data on the server

- Ability to disable unnecessary network services that may be built into the OS or server software

- Ability to control access to various forms of executable programs, such as Common Gateway Interface (CGI) scripts and server plug-ins for Web servers, if applicable

- Ability to log appropriate server activities to detect intrusions and attempted intrusions

---

[7] Content derived from Julia Allen et al., *Securing Network Servers*, April 2000, http://www.sei.cmu.edu/pub/documents/sims/pdf/sim010.pdf

- Provision of a host-based firewall capability to restrict both incoming and outgoing traffic

- Support for strong authentication protocols and encryption algorithms

In addition, organizations should consider the availability of trained, experienced staff to administer the server. Many organizations have learned the difficult lesson that a capable and experienced administrator for one type of operating environment is not automatically as effective for another.

Many servers host sensitive information, and many others, such as public-facing Web servers, should be treated as sensitive because of the damage to the organization's reputation that could occur if the servers' integrity is compromised. In such cases, it is critical that the servers are located in secure physical environments. When planning the location of a server, the following issues should be considered:

- Are the appropriate physical security protection mechanisms in place for the server and its networking components (e.g., routers, switches)? Examples include—

  - Locks

  - Card reader access

  - Security guards

  - Physical intrusion detection systems (e.g., motion sensors, cameras).

- Are there appropriate environmental controls so that the necessary humidity and temperature are maintained? If high availability is required, are there redundant environmental controls?

- Is there a backup power source? For how long will it provide power?

- Is there appropriate fire containment equipment? Does it minimize damage to equipment that would otherwise not be impacted by the fire?

- If high availability is required, are there redundant network connections? (For Internet-facing servers, this generally means Internet connections from at least two different Internet service providers [ISP].) Is there another data center that can be used to host servers in the event of a catastrophe at the original data center?

- If the location is subject to known natural disasters, is it hardened against those disasters and/or is there a contingency site outside the potential disaster area?

3.2 Security Management Staff

Because server security is tightly intertwined with the organization's general information system security posture, a number of IT and system security staff may be involved in server planning, implementation, and administration. This section provides a list of generic roles and identifies their responsibilities as they relate to server security. These roles are for the purpose of discussion and may vary by organization.

3.2.1 Chief Information Officer

The Chief Information Officer (CIO) ensures that the organization's security posture is adequate. The CIO provides direction and advisory services for the protection of information systems for the entire organization. The CIO is responsible for the following activities associated with servers:

- Coordinating the development and maintenance of the organization's information security policies, standards, and procedures

- Coordinating the development and maintenance of the organization's change control and management procedures

- Ensuring the establishment of, and compliance with, consistent IT security policies for departments throughout the organization.

3.2.2 Information Systems Security Program Managers

The Information Systems Security Program Managers (ISSPM) oversee the implementation of and compliance with the standards, rules, and regulations specified in the organization's security policy. The ISSPMs are responsible for the following activities associated with servers:

- Ensuring that security procedures are developed and implemented

- Ensuring that security policies, standards, and requirements are followed

- Ensuring that all critical systems are identified and that contingency planning, disaster recovery plans, and continuity of operations plans exist for these critical systems

- Ensuring that critical systems are identified and scheduled for periodic security testing according to the security policy requirements of each respective system.

3.2.3 Information Systems Security Officers

Information Systems Security Officers (ISSO) are responsible for overseeing all aspects of information security within a specific organizational entity. They ensure that the organization's information security practices comply with organizational and departmental policies, standards, and procedures. ISSOs are responsible for the following activities associated with servers:

- Developing internal security standards and procedures for the servers and supporting network infrastructure

- Cooperating in the development and implementation of security tools, mechanisms, and mitigation techniques

- Maintaining standard configuration profiles for the servers and supporting network infrastructure controlled by the organization, including, but not limited to, OSs, firewalls, routers, and server applications

- Maintaining operational integrity of systems by conducting security tests and ensuring that designated IT professionals are conducting scheduled testing on critical systems.

3.2.4 Server, Network, and Security Administrators

Server administrators are system architects responsible for the overall design, implementation, and maintenance of a server. Network administrators are responsible for the overall design, implementation, and maintenance of a network. Security administrators are dedicated to performing information security functions for servers and other hosts, as well as networks. Organizations that have a dedicated information security team usually have security administrators. On a daily basis, server, network, and security administrators contend with the security requirements of the specific systems for which they are responsible. Security issues and solutions can originate from either outside (e.g., security patches and fixes from the manufacturer or computer security incident response teams) or within the organization (e.g., the security office). The administrators are responsible for the following activities associated with servers:

- Installing and configuring systems in compliance with the organizational security policies and standard system and network configurations

- Maintaining systems in a secure manner, including frequent backups and timely application of patches

- Monitoring system integrity, protection levels, and security-related events

- Following up on detected security anomalies associated with their information system resources

- Conducting security tests as required.

3.3 Management Practices

Appropriate management practices are critical to operating and maintaining a secure server. Security practices entail the identification of an organization's information system assets and the development, documentation, and implementation of policies, standards, procedures, and guidelines that ensure confidentiality, integrity, and availability of information system resources.

To ensure the security of a server and the supporting network infrastructure, organizations should implement the following practices:

- **Organizational Information System Security Policy**—A security policy should specify the basic information system security tenets and rules, and their intended internal purpose. The policy should also outline who in the organization is responsible for particular areas of information security (e.g., implementation, enforcement, audit, review). The policy must be enforced consistently throughout the organization to be effective. Generally, the CIO is responsible for drafting the organization's security policy.

- **Configuration/Change Control and Management**—The process of controlling modification to a system's design, hardware, firmware, and software provides sufficient assurance that the system is protected against the introduction of an improper modification before, during, and after system implementation. Configuration control leads to consistency with the organization's information system security policy. Configuration control is traditionally overseen by a configuration control board that is the final authority on all proposed changes to an information system. If resources allow, consider the use of development, quality assurance, and/or test environments so that changes can be vetted and tested before deployment in production.

- **Risk Assessment and Management**—Risk assessment is the process of analyzing and interpreting risk. It involves determining an assessment's scope and methodology, collecting and analyzing risk-related data, and interpreting the risk analysis results. Collecting and analyzing risk data requires identifying assets, threats, vulnerabilities, safeguards, consequences, and the probability of a successful attack. Risk management is the process of selecting and implementing controls to reduce risk to a level acceptable to the organization.

- **Standardized Configurations**—Organizations should develop standardized secure configurations for widely used OSs and server software. This will provide recommendations to server and network administrators on how to configure their systems securely and ensure consistency and compliance with the organizational security policy. Because it only takes one insecurely configured host to compromise a network, organizations with a significant number of hosts are especially encouraged to apply this recommendation.

- **Secure Programming Practices**—Organizations should adopt secure application development guidelines to ensure that they develop their applications for servers in a sufficiently secure manner.

- **Security Awareness and Training**—A security training program is critical to the overall security posture of an organization. Making users and administrators aware of their security responsibilities and teaching the correct practices helps them change their behavior to conform to security best practices. Training also supports individual accountability, which is an important method for improving information system security. If the user community includes members of the general public, providing security awareness specifically targeting them might also be appropriate.

- **Contingency, Continuity of Operations, and Disaster Recovery Planning**—Contingency plans, continuity of operations plans, and disaster recovery plans are established in advance to allow an organization or facility to maintain operations in the event of a disruption.[8]

- **Certification and Accreditation**—Certification in the context of information system security means that a system has been analyzed to determine how well it meets all of the security requirements of the organization. Accreditation occurs when the organization's management accepts that the system meets the organization's security requirements.[9]

3.4 System Security Plan

The objective of system security planning is to improve protection of information system resources.[10] Plans that adequately protect information assets require managers and information owners—directly affected by and interested in the information and/or processing capabilities—to be convinced that their information assets are adequately protected from loss, misuse, unauthorized access or modification, unavailability, and undetected activities.

The purpose of the system security plan is to provide an overview of the security and privacy requirements of the system and describe the controls in place or planned for meeting those requirements. The system security plan also delineates responsibilities and expected behavior of all individuals who access the system. The system security plan should be viewed as documentation of the structured process

---

[8] For more information, see NIST SP 800-34, *Contingency Planning Guide for Information Technology Systems* (http://csrc.nist.gov/publications/PubsSPs.html).

[9] For more information on certification and accreditation, see NIST SP 800-37, *Federal Guidelines for the Security Certification and Accreditation of Information Technology Systems* (http://csrc.nist.gov/publications/PubsSPs.html).

[10] Material in this subsection is derived from NIST SP 800-18 Revision 1, *Guide for Developing Security Plans for Federal Information Systems* (http://csrc.nist.gov/publications/PubsSPs.html).

of planning adequate, cost-effective security protection for a system. It should reflect input from various managers with responsibilities concerning the system, including information owners, the system owner, and the ISSPM.

For Federal agencies, all information systems must be covered by a system security plan. Other organizations should strongly consider the completion of a system security plan for each of their systems as well. The information system owner[11] is generally the party responsible for ensuring that the security plan is developed and maintained and that the system is deployed and operated according to the agreed-upon security requirements.

In general, an effective system security plan should include the following:

- **System Identification**—The first sections of the system security plan provide basic identifying information about the system. They contain general information such as the key points of contact for the system, the purpose of the system, the sensitivity level of the system, and the environment in which the system is deployed, including the network environment, the system's placement on the network, and the system's relationships with other systems.

- **Controls**—This section of the plan describes the control measures (in place or planned) that are intended to meet the protection requirements of the information system. Controls fall into three general categories:

    - Management controls, which focus on the management of the computer security system and the management of risk for a system.

    - Operational controls, which are primarily implemented and executed by people (rather than systems). They often require technical or specialized expertise, and often rely upon management activities as well as technical controls.

    - Technical controls, which are security mechanisms that the computer system employs. The controls can provide automated protection from unauthorized access or misuse, facilitate detection of security violations, and support security requirements for applications and data. The implementation of technical controls, however, always requires significant operational considerations and should be consistent with the management of security within the organization.[12]

3.5 Human Resources Requirements

The greatest challenge and expense in developing and securely maintaining a server is providing the necessary human resources to adequately perform the required functions. Many organizations fail to fully recognize the amount of expense and skills required to field a secure server. This failure often results in overworked employees and insecure systems. From the initial planning stages, organizations need to determine the necessary human resource requirements. Appropriate and sufficient human resources are

---

[11] The information system owner is responsible for defining the system's operating parameters, authorized functions, and security requirements. The information owner for information stored within, processed by, or transmitted by a system may or may not be the same as the information system owner. In addition, a single system may use information from multiple information owners.

[12] For more detail on management, operational, and technical controls, see NIST SP 800-53 Revision 2, *Recommended Security Controls for Federal Information Systems*, and NIST SP 800-100, *Information Security Handbook: A Guide for Managers* (http://csrc.nist.gov/publications/PubsSPs.html).

the single most important aspect of effective server security. Organizations should also consider the fact that, in general, technical solutions are not a substitute for skilled and experienced personnel.

When considering the human resource implications of developing and deploying a server, organizations should consider the following:

- **Required Personnel**—What types of personnel are required? Examples of possible positions are system administrators, server administrators, network administrators, and ISSOs.

- **Required Skills**—What are the required skills to adequately plan, develop, and maintain the server in a secure manner? Examples include OS administration, network administration, and programming.

- **Available Personnel**—What are the available human resources within the organization? In addition, what are their current skill sets and are they sufficient for supporting the server? Often, an organization discovers that its existing human resources are not sufficient and needs to consider the following options:

    - Train Current Staff—If personnel are available but they do not have the requisite skills, the organization may choose to train the existing staff in the skills required. Although this is an excellent option, the organization should ensure that employees meet all prerequisites for training.

    - Acquire Additional Staff—If not enough staff members are available or they do not have the requisite skills, it may be necessary to hire additional personnel or use external resources.

Once the organization has staffed the project and the server is active, it will be necessary to ensure the number and skills of the personnel are still adequate. The threat and vulnerability levels of IT systems, including servers, are constantly changing, as is the technology. This means that what is adequate today may not be tomorrow, so staffing needs should be reassessed periodically and additional training and other skills-building activities conducted as needed.

4. Securing the Server Operating System

Most commonly available servers operate on a general-purpose OS. Many security issues can be avoided if the OSs underlying the servers are configured appropriately. Because manufacturers are unaware of each organization's security needs, server administrators need to configure new servers to reflect their organizations' security requirements and reconfigure them as those requirements change. The practices recommended here are designed to help server administrators with server security configuration. Server administrators managing existing servers should confirm that their servers address the issues discussed.

The techniques for securing different OSs vary greatly; therefore, this section includes the generic procedures common in securing most OSs. Security configuration guides and checklists for many OSs are publicly available; these documents typically contain recommendations for settings stronger than the default level of security, and they may also contain step-by-step instructions for securing servers.[13] In addition, many organizations maintain their own guidelines specific to their requirements. Some automated tools also exist for securing OSs, and their use is recommended.

After planning the installation and deployment of the OS, as described in Section 3, and installing the OS, the following basic steps are necessary to secure the OS:

- Patch and update the OS

- Harden and configure the OS to address security adequately

- Install and configure additional security controls, if needed

- Test the security of the OS to ensure that the previous steps adequately addressed all security issues.

The combined result of these steps should be a reasonable level of protection for the server's OS.

4.1 Patch and Upgrade Operating System

Once an OS is installed, applying needed patches or upgrades to correct for known vulnerabilities is essential. Any known vulnerabilities an OS has should be corrected before using it to host a server or otherwise exposing it to untrusted users. To adequately detect and correct these vulnerabilities, server administrators should do the following:

- Create, document, and implement a patching process.[14]

- Identify vulnerabilities and applicable patches.[15]

- Mitigate vulnerabilities temporarily if needed and if feasible (until patches are available, tested, and installed).

- Install permanent fixes (patches, upgrades, etc.)

---

[13] Checklists and implementation guides for various operating systems and applications are available from NIST at http://checklists.nist.gov/. Also, see NIST SP 800-70, *Security Configuration Checklists Program for IT Products*, available at the same Web site, for general information about NIST's checklists program.

[14] For more information, see NIST SP 800-40 Version 2.0, *Creating a Patch and Vulnerability Management Program*, which is available at http://csrc.nist.gov/publications/PubsSPs.html. A single patch management process can be put into place for both operating systems and applications (including server software).

[15] To check for vulnerabilities in OSs, server software, and other applications, see the NIST National Vulnerability Database (NVD) at http://nvd.nist.gov/.

Administrators should ensure that servers, particularly new ones, are adequately protected during the patching process. For example, a server that is not fully patched or not configured securely could be compromised by threats if it is openly accessible while it is being patched. When preparing new servers for deployment, administrators should do either of the following:

- Keep the servers disconnected from networks or connect them only to an isolated "build" network until all patches have been transferred to the servers through out-of-band means (e.g., CDs) and installed, and the other configuration steps listed in this section have been performed.

- Place the servers on a virtual local area network (VLAN)[16] or other network segment that severely restricts what actions the hosts on it can perform and what communications can reach the hosts—only allowing those events that are necessary for patching and configuring the hosts. Do not transfer the hosts to regular network segments until all the configuration steps listed in this section have been performed.

Administrators should generally not apply patches to production servers without first testing them on another identically configured server because patches can inadvertently cause unexpected problems with proper server operation. Although administrators can configure servers to download patches automatically, the servers should not be configured to install them automatically so that they can first be tested.

4.2 Hardening and Securely Configuring the OS

Administrators should perform the following steps to harden and securely configure a server OS:

- Remove unnecessary services, applications, and network protocols

- Configure OS user authentication

- Configure resource controls appropriately.

These steps are discussed further in Sections 4.2.1 through 4.2.3. Also, for particularly high-security situations, administrators should consider configuring the OS to act as a bastion host. A bastion host has particularly strong security controls and is configured so as to offer the least functionality possible. The details of establishing a bastion host are necessarily OS-specific, so they are outside the scope of this publication.

4.2.1 Remove or Disable Unnecessary Services, Applications, and Network Protocols

Ideally, a server should be on a dedicated, single-purpose host. When configuring the OS, remove all services, applications, and network protocols (e.g., IPv4, IPv6) that are not required, and disable any such unnecessary components that cannot be removed. If possible, install the minimal OS configuration and then add, remove, or disable services, applications, and network protocols as needed. Many uninstall scripts or programs are far from perfect in completely removing all components of a service, so it is better not to install unnecessary services. Common types of services and applications that should usually be removed if not required (or disabled if they cannot be removed) include the following:

---

[16] VLANs can easily be misconfigured in ways that reduce or eliminate their effectiveness as a security control. Organizations planning to use VLANs should ensure that they are configured properly and that any configuration changes are carefully verified.

- File and printer sharing services (e.g., Windows Network Basic Input/Output System [NetBIOS] file and printer sharing, Network File System [NFS], FTP)

- Wireless networking services

- Remote control and remote access programs, particularly those that do not strongly encrypt their communications (e.g., Telnet)[17]

- Directory services (e.g., Lightweight Directory Access Protocol [LDAP], Network Information System [NIS])

- Web servers and services

- Email services (e.g., SMTP)

- Language compilers and libraries

- System development tools

- System and network management tools and utilities, including Simple Network Management Protocol (SNMP).

Removing unnecessary services and applications is preferable to simply disabling them through configuration settings because attacks that attempt to alter settings and activate a disabled service cannot succeed when the functional components are completely removed. Disabled services could also be enabled inadvertently through human error.

Removing or disabling unnecessary services enhances the security of a server in several ways:[18]

- Other services cannot be compromised and used to attack the host or impair the services of the server. Each service added to a host increases the risk of compromise for that host because each service is another possible avenue of access for an attacker. Less is more secure in this case.

- Other services may have defects or may be incompatible with the server itself. By removing or disabling them, they should not affect the server and should potentially improve its availability.

- The host can be configured to better suit the requirements of the particular service. Different services might require different hardware and software configurations, which could lead to unnecessary vulnerabilities or negatively affect performance.

- By reducing services, the number of logs and log entries is reduced; therefore, detecting unexpected behavior becomes easier (see Section 6.1).

Organizations should determine the services to be enabled on a server. Additional services that might be installed include web servers, database access protocols, file transfer protocols, and remote administration services. These services may be required in certain instances, but they may increase the risks to the server. Whether the risks outweigh the benefits is a decision for each organization to make.

---

[17] If a remote control or remote access program is absolutely required and it does not strongly encrypt its communications, it should be tunneled over a protocol that provides encryption, such as secure shell (SSH) or Internet Protocol Security (IPsec).

[18] Content derived from Julia Allen et al., *Securing Network Servers*, April 2000, http://www.sei.cmu.edu/pub/documents/sims/pdf/sim010.pdf

4.2.2 Configure OS User Authentication

For servers, the authorized users who can configure the OS are limited to a small number of designated server administrators. The users who can access the server, however, may range from a few authorized employees to the entire Internet community. To enforce policy restrictions, if required, the server administrator should configure the OS to authenticate a prospective user by requiring proof that the user is authorized for such access. Even if a server allows unauthenticated access to most of its services, administrative and other types of specialized access should be limited to specific individuals and groups.

Enabling authentication by the host computer involves configuring parts of the OS, firmware, and applications on the server, such as the software that implements a network service. In special situations, such as high-value/high-risk servers, organizations may also use authentication hardware, such as tokens or one-time password devices. Use of authentication mechanisms where authentication information is reusable (e.g., passwords) and transmitted in the clear over an untrusted network is strongly discouraged because the information can be intercepted and used by an attacker to masquerade as an authorized user.

To ensure the appropriate user authentication is in place, take the following steps:[19]

- **Remove or Disable Unneeded Default Accounts**—The default configuration of the OS often includes guest accounts (with and without passwords), administrator or root level accounts, and accounts associated with local and network services. The names and passwords for those accounts are well known. Remove (whenever possible) or disable unnecessary accounts to eliminate their use by attackers, including guest accounts on computers containing sensitive information. For default accounts that need to be retained, including guest accounts, severely restrict access to the accounts, including changing the names (where possible and particularly for administrator or root level accounts) and passwords to be consistent with the organizational password policy. Default account names and passwords are commonly known in the attacker community.

- **Disable Non-Interactive Accounts**—Disable accounts (and the associated passwords) that need to exist but do not require an interactive login. For Unix systems, disable the login shell or provide a login shell with NULL functionality (e.g., /bin/false).

- **Create the User Groups**—Assign users to the appropriate groups. Then assign rights to the groups, as documented in the deployment plan. This approach is preferable to assigning rights to individual users, which becomes unwieldy with large numbers of users.

- **Create the User Accounts**—The deployment plan identifies who will be authorized to use each computer and its services. Create only the necessary accounts. Permit the use of shared accounts only when no viable alternatives exist. Have ordinary user accounts for server administrators that are also users of the server.

- **Configure Automated Time Synchronization**—Some authentication protocols, such as Kerberos, will not function if the time differential between the client host and the authenticating server is significant, so servers using such protocols should be configured to automatically synchronize system time with a reliable time server. Typically the time server is internal to the organization and uses the Network Time Protocol (NTP) for synchronization; publicly available NTP servers are also available on the Internet.

---

[19] Content derived from Julia Allen et al., *Securing Network Servers*, April 2000, http://www.sei.cmu.edu/pub/documents/sims/pdf/sim010.pdf

- **Check the Organization's Password Policy**—Set account passwords appropriately. Elements that may be addressed in a password policy include the following:

    - **Length**—a minimum length for passwords.

    - **Complexity**—the mix of characters required. An example is requiring passwords to contain uppercase letters, lowercase letters, and nonalphabetic characters, and to not contain "dictionary" words.

    - **Aging**—how long a password may remain unchanged. Many policies require users and administrators to change their passwords periodically. In such cases, the frequency should be determined by the enforced length and complexity of the password, the sensitivity of the information protected, and the exposure level of passwords. If aging is required, consideration should be given to enforcing a minimum aging duration to prevent users from rapidly cycling through password changes to clear out their password history and bypass reuse restrictions.

    - **Reuse**—whether a password may be reused. Some users try to defeat a password aging requirement by changing the password to one they have used previously. If reuse is prohibited by policy, it is beneficial, if possible, to ensure that users cannot change their passwords by merely appending characters to the beginning or end of their original passwords (e.g., original password was "mysecret" and is changed to "1mysecret" or "mysecret1").

    - **Authority**—who is allowed to change or reset passwords and what sort of proof is required before initiating any changes.

    - **Password Security**—how passwords should be secured, such as not storing passwords unencrypted on the server, and requiring administrators to use different passwords for their server administration accounts than their other administration accounts.

- **Configure Computers to Prevent Password Guessing**—It is relatively easy for an unauthorized user to try to gain access to a computer by using automated software tools that attempt all passwords. If the OS provides the capability, configure it to increase the period between login attempts with each unsuccessful attempt. If that is not possible, the alternative is to deny login after a limited number of failed attempts (e.g., three). Typically, the account is "locked out" for a period of time (such as 30 minutes) or until a user with appropriate authority reactivates it.

    The choice to deny login is another situation that requires the server administrator to make a decision that balances security and convenience. Implementing this recommendation can help prevent some kinds of attacks, but it can also allow an attacker to use failed login attempts to prevent user access, resulting in a DoS condition. The risk of DoS from account lockout is much greater if the server is externally accessible and an attacker knows or can surmise a pattern to your naming convention that allows them to guess account names.

    Failed network login attempts should not prevent an authorized user or administrator from logging in at the console. Note that all failed login attempts, whether via the network or console, should be logged. If the server will not be administered remotely, disable the ability for the administrator or root level accounts to log in from the network.

- **Install and Configure Other Security Mechanisms to Strengthen Authentication**—If the information on the server requires it, consider using other authentication mechanisms such as biometrics, smart cards, client/server certificates, or one-time password systems. They can be more expensive and difficult to implement, but they may be justified in some circumstances. When such authentication mechanisms and devices are used, the organization's policy should be changed accordingly, if necessary. Some organizational policies may already require the use of strong authentication mechanisms.

As mentioned earlier, attackers using network sniffers can easily capture passwords passed across a network in clear text. However, passwords are economical and appropriate if properly protected while in transit. Organizations should implement authentication and encryption technologies, such as Secure Sockets Layer (SSL)/Transport Layer Security (TLS), Secure Shell (SSH), or virtual private networks using IPsec or SSL/TLS, to protect passwords during transmission over untrusted networks. Requiring server authentication to be used with encryption technologies reduces the likelihood of successful man-in-the-middle and spoofing attacks.

4.2.3 Configure Resource Controls Appropriately

All commonly used server OSs provide the capability to specify access privileges individually for files, directories, devices, and other computational resources. By carefully setting access controls and denying personnel unauthorized access, the server administrator can reduce intentional and unintentional security breaches. For example, denying read access to files and directories helps to protect confidentiality of information, and denying unnecessary write (modify) access can help maintain the integrity of information. Limiting the execution privilege of most system-related tools to authorized system administrators can prevent users from making configuration changes that could reduce security. It also can restrict the attacker's ability to use those tools to attack the server or other hosts on the network. Auditing should also be enabled as appropriate to monitor attempts to access protected resources.

In some cases, administrators configure the OS so as to provide an isolated virtual environment that the server software will be run within. This environment, sometimes called a sandbox or a jail, presents a limited set of real or virtual resources that the server software or its users can access. The OS is configured so that server processes and user actions cannot "break out" of the environment. A common example of an isolated virtual environment is the use of the Unix chroot command to contain anonymous FTP activity. Even if a malicious user exploited a vulnerability in the FTP service, the user would only gain access to the virtual environment and not to the underlying OS. Details on creating sandbox and jail environments are OS and server-specific, and therefore are outside the scope of this publication.

4.3 Install and Configure Additional Security Controls

OSs often do not include all of the security controls necessary to secure the OS, services, and applications adequately. In such cases, administrators need to select, install, configure, and maintain additional software to provide the missing controls. Commonly needed controls include the following:

- Anti-malware software, such as antivirus software, anti-spyware software, and rootkit detectors, to protect the local OS from malware and to detect and eradicate any infections that occur.[20] Examples of when anti-malware software would be helpful include a system administrator bringing infected media to the server and a network service worm contacting the server and infecting it.

- Host-based intrusion detection and prevention software (IDPS), to detect attacks performed against the server, including DoS attacks. For example, one form of host-based IDPS, file integrity checking software, can identify changes to critical system files.

---

[20] Additional information on anti-malware software is available from NIST SP 800-83, *Guide to Malware Incident Prevention and Handling* (http://csrc.nist.gov/publications/PubsSPs.html).

- Host-based firewalls, to protect the server from unauthorized access.[21]

- Patch management or vulnerability management software to ensure that vulnerabilities are addressed promptly. Patch management and vulnerability management software can be used only to apply patches or also to identify new vulnerabilities in the server's OSs, services, and applications.

Some servers also use disk encryption technologies to protect their stored data from attackers who gain physical access to the servers. Disk encryption technologies are built into some operating systems, and third-party disk encryption products are also available.

When planning security controls, server administrators should consider the resources that the security controls will consume. A server's performance could degrade if it does not have enough memory and processing capacity for the controls. Server administrators should also consider any network-based security controls, such as network firewalls and intrusion detection systems, that could provide additional protection for the server. If host-based security controls are too resource-intensive for a server or are otherwise infeasible, server administrators may need to compensate by using additional network-based security controls to protect the server's OS, services, and applications. For many servers, network-based security controls are used in addition to host-based security controls to provide additional layers of security.

4.4 Security Testing the Operating System

Periodic security testing of the OS is a vital way to identify vulnerabilities and to ensure that the existing security precautions are effective and that security controls are configured properly (for example, the required cryptographic algorithms are in use to protect network communications). Common methods for testing OSs include vulnerability scanning and penetration testing. Vulnerability scanning usually entails using an automated vulnerability scanner to scan a host or group of hosts on a network for application, network, and OS vulnerabilities. Penetration testing is a testing process designed to compromise a network using the tools and methodologies of an attacker. It involves iteratively identifying and exploiting the weakest areas of the network to gain access to the remainder of the network, eventually compromising the overall security of the network. Vulnerability scanning should be conducted periodically, at least weekly to monthly, and penetration testing should be conducted at least annually. Because both of these testing techniques are also applicable to testing the server application, they are discussed in detail in Section 6.4.[22]

Factors to be considered when deciding whether to test the production server or a similarly configured non-production server include the following:

- The possible impact to the production server. For example, if a certain test technique is likely to cause a denial of service, then that technique should probably be used against the non-production server.

- The presence of sensitive personally identifiable information (PII). If testing could expose sensitive PII, such as Social Security Numbers (SSN) or credit card information, to people without authorization to see it, then organizations should consider performing the testing on a non-production server that holds a false version of the PII (e.g., test data instead of actual sensitive PII).

---

[21] For more information on firewalls, see NIST SP 800-41 Revision 1 (Draft), *Guidelines on Firewalls and Firewall Policy* (http://csrc.nist.gov/publications/PubsSPs.html).

[22] For information on other testing techniques, see NIST SP 800-115 (Draft), *Technical Guide to Information Security Testing* (http://csrc.nist.gov/publications/PubsSPs.html).

- How similarly the production and non-production servers can be configured. In practice, there are usually inconsistencies between the test and production environments, which can result in missed vulnerabilities if the non-production servers are used.

5. Securing the Server Software

Once the OS has been installed and secured, as described in Section 4, the next step is to install and secure the chosen server software, which is described in this section. Before starting this process, read the server software documentation carefully and understand the various options available during the installation process. Also, be sure to visit the server software manufacturer's Web site or a vulnerability database Web site, such as the National Vulnerability Database (NVD),[23] to determine whether there are known vulnerabilities and related patches available that should be installed or configured as part of the setup process. Only after these preliminary steps are accomplished should the installation be started. Note that this section discusses only generic installation and configuration procedures; specific directions for particular servers are available from server manufacturers and from security checklist repositories.[24]

A partially configured and/or patched server should not be exposed to external networks (e.g., the Internet) or external users. In addition, internal network access should be as limited as possible until all software is installed, patched, and configured securely. Insecure servers can be compromised in a matter of minutes after being placed on the Internet. While it is ideal to fully harden the platform before placing it on the network, it is not always feasible. For example, some application development tool combinations cannot be installed, configured, and tested on top of a pre-hardened OS and Web server configuration. In such situations, stepwise or incremental hardening is a viable option to consider, with full validation of complete hardening occurring at production deployment.

5.1 Securely Installing the Server Software

In many respects, the secure installation and configuration of the server software mirrors the OS process discussed in Section 4. The overarching principle, as before, is to install only the services required for the server and to eliminate any known vulnerabilities through patches or upgrades. Any unnecessary applications, services, or scripts that are installed should be removed immediately once the installation process is complete. During the installation of the server software, the following steps should be performed:

- Install the server software either on a dedicated host or on a dedicated guest OS if virtualization is being employed.

- Apply any patches or upgrades to correct for known vulnerabilities in the server software.

- Create a dedicated physical disk or logical partition (separate from OS and server application) for server data, if applicable.

- Remove or disable all services installed by the server application but not required (e.g., gopher, FTP, HTTP, remote administration).

- Remove or disable all unneeded default user accounts created by the server installation.

- Remove all manufacturers' documentation from the server.

- Remove all example or test files from the server, including sample content, scripts, and executable code.

---

[23] NVD is available at http://nvd.nist.gov/.
[24] NIST hosts a security checklist repository at http://checklists.nist.gov/.

- Remove all unneeded compilers.

- Apply the appropriate security template or hardening script to the server.

- For external-facing servers, reconfigure service banners not to report the server and OS type and version, if possible.[25]

- Configure warning banners for all services that support such banners.[26]

- Configure each network service to listen for client connections on only the necessary TCP and UDP ports, if possible.[27]

Organizations should consider installing the server with non-standard directory names, directory locations, and filenames if possible. Many server attack tools and worms targeting servers only look for files and directories in their default locations. While this will not stop determined attackers, it will force them to work harder to compromise the server, and it also increases the likelihood of attack detection because of the failed attempts to access the default filenames and directories and the additional time needed to perform an attack.

5.2 Configuring Access Controls

Most server OSs provide the capability to specify access privileges individually for files, devices, and other computational resources on that host. Any information that the server can access using these controls can potentially be distributed to all users accessing the server. The server software is likely to include mechanisms to provide additional file, device, and resource access controls specific to its operation. It is important to set identical permissions for both the OS and server application; otherwise, too much or too little access may be granted to users. Server administrators should consider how best to configure access controls to protect information stored on servers from two perspectives:

- Limit the access of the server application to a subset of computational resources.

- Limit the access of users through additional access controls enforced by the server, where more detailed levels of access control are required.

The proper setting of access controls can help prevent the disclosure of sensitive or restricted information that is not intended for public dissemination. In addition, access controls can be used to limit resource use in the event of a DoS attack against the server. Similarly, access controls can enforce separation of duty by ensuring server logs cannot be modified by server administrators and potentially ensure that the server process is only allowed to append to the log files.

Typical files to which access should be controlled are as follows:

- Application software and configuration files

- Files related directly to security mechanisms:

---

[25] This deters novice attackers and some forms of malware, but it will not deter more skilled attackers from identifying the server and OS type.
[26] If the organization does not already have approved standard warning banner text, work with the organization's legal counsel to develop suitable banner text.
[27] Content derived from Julia Allen et al., *Securing Network Servers*, April 2000, http://www.sei.cmu.edu/pub/documents/sims/pdf/sim010.pdf

- Password hash files and other files used in authentication
- Files containing authorization information used in controlling access
- Cryptographic key material used in confidentiality, integrity, and non-repudiation services

- Server log and system audit files
- System software and configuration files
- Server content files.

It is vital that the server application executes only under a unique individual user and group identity with very restrictive access controls. New user and group identities should be established for exclusive use by the server software. The new user and new group should be independent from all other users and groups and unique. This is a prerequisite for implementing the access controls described in the following steps. During initialization, the server may have to run with root (Unix) or administrator/system (Windows) privileges; ensure that the server is configured to reduce its privileges to those of the server user after performing its initialization functions.

In addition, use the server OS to limit which files can be accessed by the service processes. These processes should have read-only access to those files necessary to perform the service and should have no access to other files, such as server log files. Use server host OS access controls to enforce the following:[28]

- Service processes are configured to run as a user with a strictly limited set of privileges (i.e., not running as root, administrator, or equivalent).

- Service processes can only write to server content files and directories if necessary.

- Temporary files created by the server software are restricted to a specified and appropriately protected subdirectory (if possible). Access to these temporary files is limited to the server processes that created the files (if possible).

It may also be necessary to ensure that the server software cannot save (or, in some cases, read) files outside the specified file structure dedicated to server content. This may be a configuration choice in the server software, or it may be a choice in how the server process is controlled by the OS. Ensure that such directories and files (outside the specified directory tree) cannot be accessed both directly and through the server software.

5.3 Server Resource Constraints

To mitigate the effects of certain types of DoS attacks, configure the server to limit the amount of OS resources it can consume. Some examples include—

- Installing server content on a different hard drive or logical partition than the OS and server software.

---

[28] Derived from Klaus-Peter Kossakowski and Julia Allen, *Securing Public Web Servers*, 2000, http://www.sei.cmu.edu/pub/documents/sims/pdf/sim011.pdf. Its recommendations are specific to Web servers, but the same principles apply to any type of server.

- Placing a limit on the amount of hard drive space that is dedicated for uploads, if uploads to the server are allowed. Ideally, uploads should be placed on a separate partition to provide stronger assurance that the hard drive limit cannot be exceeded.

- If uploads are allowed to the server, ensuring that these files are not readable by the server until after some automated or manual review process is used to screen them. This measure prevents the server from being used to propagate malware or traffic pirated software, attack tools, pornography, etc. It is also possible to limit the size of each uploaded file, which could limit the potential effects of a DoS attack involving uploading many large files.

- Ensuring that log files are stored in a location that is sized appropriately. Ideally, log files should be stored on a separate partition. If an attack causes the size of the log files to increase beyond acceptable limits, a physical partition helps ensure the server has enough resources to handle the situation appropriately.

- Configuring the maximum number of server processes and/or network connections that the server should allow.

To some degree, these actions protect against attacks that attempt to fill the file system on the server OS with extraneous and incorrect information that may cause the server to crash. Logging information generated by the server OS may help in recognizing such attacks. As discussed in Section 6.1, administrators should store server logs on centralized logging servers whenever possible and also store logs locally if feasible. If an attack causes the server to be compromised, the attacker could modify or erase locally stored logs to conceal information on the attack. Maintaining a copy of the logs on a centralized logging server gives administrators more information to use when investigating such a compromise.

In addition to the controls mentioned above, it is often necessary to configure timeouts and other controls to further reduce the impact of certain DoS attacks. One type of DoS attack takes advantage of the practical limits on simultaneous network connections by quickly establishing connections up to the maximum permitted, such that no new legitimate users can gain access. By setting network connection timeouts (the time after which an inactive connection is dropped) to a minimum acceptable time limit, established connections will time out as quickly as possible, opening up new connections to legitimate users. This measure only mitigates the effects; it does not defeat the attack.

If the maximum number of open connections (or connections that are half-open—that is, the first part of the TCP handshake was successful) is set to a low number, an attacker can easily consume the available connections with illegitimate requests (often called a SYN flood). Setting the maximum to a much higher number may mitigate the effect of such an attack, but at the expense of consuming additional resources. Note that this is only an issue for servers that are not protected by a firewall that stops SYN flood attacks. Most enterprise-level firewalls protect servers from SYN floods by intercepting them before they reach the servers.

5.4 Selecting and Implementing Authentication and Encryption Technologies

Many servers support a range of technologies for identifying and authenticating users with differing privileges for accessing information. Without user authentication, a server cannot restrict access to authorized users—all services and information will be accessible by anyone with access to the server. In many cases, this is not acceptable. Encryption can be used to protect information traversing the connection between a server and a client. Without encryption, anyone with access to the network traffic can determine, and possibly alter, the content of sensitive information, even if the user accessing the information has been authenticated. This may violate the confidentiality and integrity of critical information.

Organizations should periodically examine the services and information accessible on the server and determine the necessary security requirements. While doing so, the organization should identify information that shares the same security and protection requirements. For sensitive information, the organization should determine the users or user groups that should have access to each set of resources. For information that requires some level of user authentication, the organization should determine which authentication technologies or methods would provide the appropriate level of authentication and encryption. Each has its own unique benefits and costs that should be weighed carefully with client and organizational requirements and policies. It may be desirable to use some authentication methods in combination. NIST SP 800-63, *Electronic Authentication Guideline*, contains additional information on authentication mechanisms.

Federal government organizations are required to use Federal Information Processing Standards (FIPS)-validated cryptographic implementations when using cryptography to protect stored data and data communications. The Cryptographic Module Validation Program (CMVP) performs validation testing of cryptographic modules.[29] NIST provides a list of FIPS 140 compliant[30] manufacturers and implementations.[31] Additional information on encrypting communications is available from NIST SP 800-52, *Guidelines for the Selection and Use of Transport Layer Security (TLS) Implementations*, NIST SP 800-77, *Guide to IPsec VPNs*, and NIST SP 800-113, *Guide to SSL VPNs*.[32]

Organizations should be prepared to migrate their servers to stronger cryptographic technologies over time as weaknesses are identified in the servers' existing cryptographic technologies. For example, NIST has recommended that use of the Secure Hash Algorithm 1 (SHA-1) be phased out by 2010 in favor of SHA-224, SHA-256, and other larger, stronger hash functions.[33] Organizations should stay aware of cryptographic requirements and recommendations and plan to update their servers accordingly.

---

[29] http://csrc.nist.gov/groups/STM/index.html
[30] As of this writing, the current version of FIPS 140 is 140-2, *Security Requirements for Cryptographic Modules* (http://csrc.nist.gov/publications/fips/fips140-2/fips1402.pdf). FIPS 140-3 is currently available in draft (http://csrc.nist.gov/publications/PubsFIPS.html).
[31] http://csrc.nist.gov/groups/STM/cmvp/documents/140-1/1401vend.htm
[32] All of these NIST SPs are available at http://csrc.nist.gov/publications/PubsSPs.html.
[33] See http://csrc.nist.gov/groups/ST/hash/index.html, FIPS PUB 180-2, *Secure Hash Standard*, http://csrc.nist.gov/publications/fips/fips180-2/fips180-2withchangenotice.pdf, and FIPS PUB 180-3 (Draft), http://csrc.nist.gov/publications/PubsFIPS.html for additional information on hash function requirements.

6. Maintaining the Security of the Server

After initially deploying a server, administrators need to maintain its security continuously. This section provides general recommendations for securely administering servers. Vital activities include handling and analyzing log files, performing regular server backups, recovering from server compromises, testing server security regularly, and performing remote administration securely. As discussed in Section 4, security configuration guides and checklists are publicly available for many OSs and server software; many of these documents contain OS and server-specific recommendations for security maintenance. Other maintenance activities discussed in earlier sections, and thus not duplicated here, include testing and deploying OS and server patches and updates, maintaining the secure configuration of the OS and server software, and maintaining additional security controls used for the server.[34]

6.1 Logging

Logging is a cornerstone of a sound security posture. Capturing the correct data in the logs and then monitoring those logs closely is vital.[35] Network and system logs are important, especially system logs in the case of encrypted communications, where network monitoring is less effective. Server software can provide additional log data relevant to server-specific events.

Reviewing logs is mundane and reactive, and many server administrators devote their time to performing duties that they consider more important or urgent. However, log files are often the only record of suspicious behavior. Enabling the mechanisms to log information allows the logs to be used to detect failed and successful intrusion attempts and to initiate alert mechanisms when further investigation is needed. Procedures and tools need to be in place to process and analyze the log files and to review alert notifications.

Server logs provide—

- Alerts to suspicious activities that require further investigation

- Tracking of an attacker's activities

- Assistance in the recovery of the server

- Assistance in post-event investigation

- Required information for legal proceedings.

The selection and implementation of specific server software determines which actions the server administrator should perform to establish logging configurations. Some of the information contained in the steps below may not be fully applicable to all server software products.

6.1.1 Identifying Logging Capabilities and Requirements

Each type of server software supports different logging capabilities. Some server software may use a single log, while other server software may use multiple logs (each for different types of records). Some

---

[34] This includes both host-based and network-based security controls. However, in many environments, network-based security controls such as enterprise firewalls and intrusion detection systems are maintained by someone other than the server administrator.
[35] For more information on logging, see NIST SP 800-92, *Guide to Computer Security Log Management*, which is available at http://csrc.nist.gov/publications/PubsSPs.html.

server software permits administrators to select from multiple log formats, such as proprietary, database, and delimiter-separated.

If a server supports the execution of programs, scripts, or plug-ins, it may be necessary for the programs, scripts, or plug-ins to perform additional logging. Often, critical events take place within the application code itself and will not be logged by the server. If server administrators develop or acquire application programs, scripts, or plug-ins, it is strongly recommended that they define and implement a comprehensive and easy-to-understand logging approach based on the logging mechanisms provided by the server host OS. Log information associated with programs, scripts, and plug-ins can add significantly to the typical information logged by the server and may prove invaluable when investigating events.

Ensuring that sufficient log capacity is available is a concern because logs often take considerably more space than administrators initially estimate, especially when logging is set to a highly detailed level. Administrators should closely monitor the size of the log files when they implement different logging settings to ensure that the log files do not fill up the allocated storage. Because of the size of the log files, removing and archiving the logs more frequently or reducing the logging level of detail may be necessary.

Some server programs provide a capability to enforce or disable the checking of specified access controls during program startup. This level of control may be helpful, for example, to avoid inadvertent alteration of log files because of errors in file access administration. Server administrators should determine the circumstances under which they may wish to enable such checks (assuming the server software supports this feature).

All servers should use time synchronization technologies, such as the Network Time Protocol (NTP), to keep their internal clocks synchronized with an accurate time source. This provides accurate timestamps for logs.

6.1.2 Reviewing and Retaining Log Files

Reviewing log files is a tedious and time-consuming task that informs administrators of events that have already occurred. Accordingly, files are often useful for corroborating other evidence, such as a CPU utilization spike or anomalous network traffic reported by an IDPS. When a log is used to corroborate other evidence, a focused review is in order. For example, if an IDPS reported a suspicious outbound FTP connection from a Web server at 8:17 a.m., then a review of the logs generated around 8:17 a.m. is appropriate. Server logs should also be reviewed for indications of attacks. The frequency of the reviews depends on the following factors:

- Amount of traffic the server receives

- General threat level (certain servers receive many more attacks than other servers and thus should have their logs reviewed more frequently)

- Specific threats (at certain times, specific threats arise that may require more frequent log file analysis)

- Vulnerability of the server

- Value of data and services provided by the server.

Reviews should take place regularly (e.g., daily) and when a suspicious activity has been noted or a threat warning has been issued. Obviously, the task could quickly become burdensome to a server administrator. To reduce this burden, automated log analysis tools have been developed (see Section 6.1.3).

In addition, a long-term and more in-depth analysis of the logs is needed. Because a server attack can involve hundreds of unique requests, an attacker may attempt to disguise a server attack by increasing the interval between requests. In this case, reviewing a single day's or week's logs may not show recognizable trends. However, when trends are analyzed over a week, month, or quarter, multiple attacks from the same host or subnet can be more easily recognized.

Log files should be protected to ensure that if an attacker does compromise a server, the log files cannot be altered to cover the attack. Although encryption can be useful in protecting log files, the best solution is to store log files on a host separate from the server. This is often called a centralized logging server. Centralized logging is often performed using syslog, which is a standard logging protocol.[36] Alternately, some organizations use security information and event management (SIEM) software that uses centralized servers to perform log analysis, database servers to store logs, and either agents installed on the individual hosts or processes running on the centralized servers to transfer server logs or log data from the hosts to the servers and parse the logs.[37]

Log files should be backed up and archived regularly. Archiving log files for a period of time is important for several reasons, including supporting certain legal actions and troubleshooting problems with the server. The retention period for archived log files depends on a number of factors, including the following:

- Legal and regulatory requirements

- Organizational requirements

- Size of logs (which is directly related to the traffic of the site and the number of details logged)

- Value of server data and services

- Threat level.

6.1.3 Automated Log File Analysis Tools

Many servers receive significant amounts of traffic, and the log files quickly become voluminous. Automated log analysis tools should be installed to ease the burden on server administrators. These tools analyze the entries in the server log files and identify suspicious and unusual activity. As mentioned in Section 6.1.2, some organizations use SIEM software for centralized logging, which can also perform automated log file analysis. Many commercial and public domain tools are also available to support regular analysis of particular types of server logs.

The automated log analyzer should forward any suspicious events to the responsible server administrator or security incident response team as soon as possible for follow-up investigation. Some organizations

---

[36] Syslog is defined in IETF RFC 3164, *The BSD Syslog Protocol*, which is available at http://www.ietf.org/rfc/rfc3164.txt.
[37] More information on syslog and SIEM implementations is provided in NIST SP 800-92, *Guide to Computer Security Log Management*, which is available at http://csrc.nist.gov/publications/PubsSPs.html.

may wish to use two or more log analyzers, which will reduce the risk of missing an attacker or other significant events in the log files.[38]

6.2 Server Backup Procedures

One of the most important functions of a server administrator is to maintain the integrity of the data on the server. This is important because servers are often some of the most exposed and vital hosts on an organization's network. The server administrator needs to perform backups of the server on a regular basis for several reasons. A server could fail as a result of a malicious or unintentional act or a hardware or software failure. In addition, Federal agencies and many other organizations are governed by regulations on the backup and archiving of server data. Server data should also be backed up regularly for legal and financial reasons.

6.2.1 Server Data Backup Policies

All organizations need to create a server data backup policy. Three main factors influence the contents of this policy:

- Legal requirements
    - Applicable laws and regulations (Federal, state, and international)
    - Litigation requirements
- Mission requirements
    - Contractual
    - Accepted practices
    - Criticality of data to organization
- Organizational guidelines and policies.

Although each organization's server backup policy will be different to reflect its particular environment, it should address the following issues:

- Purpose of the policy
- Parties affected by the policy
- Servers covered by the policy
- Definitions of key terms, especially legal and technical
- Detailed requirements from the legal, business, and organization's perspective
- Required frequency of backups

---

[38] Derived from Karen Kent and Murugiah Souppaya, NIST SP 800-92, *Guide to Computer Security Log Management*, April 2006, http://csrc.nist.gov/publications/PubsSPs.html

- Procedures for ensuring data is properly retained and protected

- Procedures for ensuring data is properly destroyed or archived when no longer required

- Procedures for preserving information for Freedom of Information Act (FOIA) requests, legal investigations, and other such requests

- Responsibilities of those involved in data retention, protection, and destruction activities

- Retention period for each type of information logged

- Specific duties of a central/organizational data backup team, if one exists.

6.2.2 Server Backup Types

Three primary types of backups exist: full, incremental, and differential. Full backups include the OS, applications, and data stored on the server (i.e., an image of every piece of data stored on the server hard drives). The advantage of a full backup is that it is easy to restore the entire server to the state (e.g., configuration, patch level, data) it was in when the backup was performed. The disadvantage of full backups is that they take considerable time and resources to perform. Incremental backups reduce the impact of backups by backing up only data that has changed since the previous backup (either full or incremental).

Differential backups reduce the number of backup sets that must be accessed to restore a configuration by backing up all changed data since the last full backup. However, each differential backup increases as time lapses from the last full backup, requiring more processing time and storage than would an incremental backup. Generally, full backups are performed less frequently (weekly to monthly or when a significant change occurs), and incremental or differential backups are performed more frequently (daily to weekly). The frequency of backups will be determined by several factors:

- Volatility of information on the site

    - Static content (less frequent backups)

    - Dynamic content (more frequent backups)

    - E-commerce/e-government (very frequent backups)

- Volatility of configuring the server

- Type of data to be backed up (e.g., system, application, log, or user data)

- Amount of data to be backed up

- Backup device and media available

- Time available for dumping backup data

- Criticality of data

- Threat level faced by the server

- Effort required for data reconstruction without data backup

- Other data backup or redundancy features of the server (e.g., Redundant Array of Inexpensive Disks [RAID]).

For servers with highly dynamic data, standard backups may be insufficient to ensure the availability of the server data. Some services have data modified on a continuous basis, and a server failure necessitating restoration from a backup would cause the loss of all data changes made since the previous backup. Some servers offer replication services that allow data changes from one server to be duplicated on another server, either for individual changes or small batches of changes. Replication does place additional load on servers and networks, so organizations need to weigh the costs of replication against the costs of lost availability should a server failure occur. Replication is not intended to take the place of standard backups, only to provide a capability to duplicate recent changes to data.

6.2.3 Maintain a Test Server

Most organizations will probably wish to maintain a test or development server for their most important servers, at a minimum.[39] Ideally, this server should have hardware and software identical to the production or live server and be located on an internal network segment (intranet) where it can be fully protected by the organization's perimeter network defenses. Although the cost of maintaining an additional server is not inconsequential, having a test server offers numerous advantages:

- It provides a platform to test new patches and service packs before application on the production server.

- It provides a development platform for the server administrator to develop and test new content and applications.

- It provides a platform to test configuration settings before applying them to production servers.

- Software critical for development and testing but that might represent an unacceptable security risk on the production server can be installed on the development server (e.g., software compliers, administrative tool kits, remote access software).

6.3 Recovering From a Security Compromise

Most organizations eventually face a successful compromise of one or more hosts on their network. Organizations should create and document the required policies and procedures for responding to successful intrusions.[40] The response procedures should outline the actions that are required to respond to a successful compromise of the server and the appropriate sequence of these actions (sequence can be critical). Most organizations already have a dedicated incident response team in place, which should be contacted immediately when there is suspicion or confirmation of a compromise. In addition, the

---

[39] Larger organizations sometimes have several test and development servers and environments for their most critical servers and systems. For example, there could be a server for developer testing, another server for quality assurance testing, and one or more externally accessible servers for testing from business partners.

[40] For more information on this area, see NIST SP 800-61 Revision 1, *Computer Security Incident Handling Guide*, and NIST SP 800-18 Revision 1, *Guide for Developing Security Plans for Federal Information Systems* (http://csrc.nist.gov/publications/PubsSPs.html).

organization may wish to ensure that some of its staff are knowledgeable in the fields of computer and network forensics.[41]

A server administrator should follow the organization's policies and procedures for incident handling, and the incident response team should be contacted for guidance before the organization takes any action after a suspected or confirmed security compromise. Examples of steps commonly performed after discovering a successful compromise are as follows:

- Report the incident to the organization's computer incident response capability.

- Isolate the compromised systems or take other steps to contain the attack so that additional information can be collected.[42]

- Consult expeditiously, as appropriate, with management, legal counsel, and law enforcement.

- Investigate similar[43] hosts to determine if the attacker also has compromised other systems.

- Analyze the intrusion, including—

    - The current state of the server, starting with the most ephemeral data (e.g., current network connections, memory dump, files time stamps, logged in users)

    - Modifications made to the server's software and configuration

    - Modifications made to the data

    - Tools or data left behind by the attacker

    - System, intrusion detection, and firewall log files.

- Restore the server before redeploying it.

    - Either install a clean version of the OS, applications, necessary patches, and server content; or restore the server from backups (this option can be more risky because the backups may have been made after the compromise, and restoring from a compromised backup may still allow the attacker access to the server).

    - Disable unnecessary services.

    - Apply all patches.

    - Change all passwords (including on uncompromised hosts, if their passwords are believed to have been seen by the compromised server, or if the same passwords are used on other hosts).

---

[41] More information on computer and network forensics is available from NIST SP 800-86, *Guide to Integrating Forensic Techniques Into Incident Response* (http://csrc.nist.gov/publications/PubsSPs.html).
[42] Isolating the server must be accomplished with great care if the organization wishes to collect evidence. Many attackers configure compromised systems to erase evidence if a compromised system is disconnected from the network or rebooted. One method to isolate a server would be to reconfigure the nearest upstream switch or router.
[43] Similar hosts would include hosts that are in the same IP address range, have the same or similar passwords, share a trust relationship, and/or have the same OS and/or applications.

- Reconfigure network security elements (e.g., firewall, router, IDPS) to provide additional protection and notification.

- Test the server to ensure security.

- Reconnect the server to the network.

- Monitor the server and network for signs that the attacker is attempting to access the server or network again.

- Document lessons learned.

Based on the organization's policy and procedures, system administrators should decide whether to reinstall the OS of a compromised server or restore it from a backup. Factors that are often considered include the following:

- Level of access that the attacker gained (e.g., root, user, guest, system)

- Type of attacker (internal or external)

- Purpose of compromise (e.g., Web page defacement, illegal software repository, platform for other attacks, data exfiltration)

- Method used for the server compromise

- Actions of the attacker during and after the compromise (e.g., log files, intrusion detection reports)

- Duration of the compromise

- Extent of the compromise on the network (e.g., the number of hosts compromised)

- Results of consultation with management and legal counsel.

The lower the level of access gained by the intruder and the more the server administrator understands about the attacker's actions, the less risk there is in restoring from a backup and patching the vulnerability. For incidents in which there is less known about the attacker's actions and/or in which the attacker gains high-level access, it is recommended that the OS, server software, and other applications be reinstalled from the manufacturer's original distribution media and that the server data be restored only from a known good backup.

If legal action is pursued, server administrators need to be aware of the guidelines for handling a host after a compromise. Consult legal counsel and relevant law enforcement authorities as appropriate.

6.4 Security Testing Servers

Periodic security testing of servers is critical. Without periodic testing, there is no assurance that current protective measures are working or that the security patch applied by the server administrator is functioning as advertised. Although a variety of security testing techniques exists, vulnerability scanning is the most common. Vulnerability scanning assists a server administrator in identifying vulnerabilities and verifying whether the existing security measures are effective. Penetration testing is also used, but it is used less frequently and usually only as part of an overall penetration test of the organization's network.[44]

6.4.1 Vulnerability Scanning

Vulnerability scanners are automated tools that are used to identify vulnerabilities and misconfigurations of hosts. Many vulnerability scanners also provide information about mitigating discovered vulnerabilities. Vulnerability scanners attempt to identify vulnerabilities in the hosts scanned. Vulnerability scanners can help identify out-of-date software versions, missing patches, or system upgrades, and they can validate compliance with or deviations from the organization's security policy. To accomplish this, vulnerability scanners identify OSs, server software, and other major software applications running on hosts and match them with known vulnerabilities in their vulnerability databases.

However, vulnerability scanners have some significant weaknesses. Generally, they identify only surface vulnerabilities and are unable to address the overall risk level of a scanned server. Although the scan process itself is highly automated, vulnerability scanners can have a high false positive error rate (reporting vulnerabilities when none exist). Also, vulnerability scanners may not be able to recognize that compensating controls are in place that mitigate a detected vulnerability. This means an individual with expertise in server security and administration must interpret the results. Furthermore, vulnerability scanners cannot generally identify vulnerabilities in custom code or applications.

Vulnerability scanners rely on periodic updating of the vulnerability database to recognize the latest vulnerabilities. Before running any scanner, server administrators should install the latest updates to its vulnerability database. Some databases are updated more regularly than others (the frequency of updates should be a major consideration when choosing a vulnerability scanner). Because of the potential negative impact of vulnerability scanning, server administrators may wish to scan test servers first with new vulnerability database updates to ascertain their impact on the servers before scanning production servers.

Vulnerability scanners are often better at detecting well known vulnerabilities than more esoteric ones because it is impossible for any one scanning product to incorporate all known vulnerabilities in a timely manner. In addition, manufacturers want to keep the speed of their scanners high (the more vulnerabilities detected, the more tests required, which slows the overall scanning process). Therefore, vulnerability scanners may be less useful to server administrators operating less popular servers, OSs, or custom-coded applications.

Vulnerability scanners provide the following capabilities:

- Identifying active hosts on a network

- Identifying active services (ports) on hosts and which of these are vulnerable

- Identifying applications and banner grabbing

- Identifying OSs

- Identifying vulnerabilities associated with discovered OSs, server software, and other applications

- Testing compliance with host application usage/security policies.

---

[44] For information about other testing techniques, see NIST SP 800-115 (Draft), *Technical Guide to Information Security Testing* (http://csrc.nist.gov/publications/PubsSPs.html).

Organizations should conduct vulnerability scanning to validate that OSs and server software are up-to-date on security patches and software versions. Vulnerability scanning is a labor-intensive activity that requires a high degree of human involvement to interpret the results. It may also be disruptive to operations by taking up network bandwidth, slowing network response times, and potentially affecting the availability of the scanned server or its applications. However, vulnerability scanning is extremely important for ensuring that vulnerabilities are mitigated as soon as possible, before they are discovered and exploited by adversaries. Vulnerability scanning should be conducted on a weekly to monthly basis. Many organizations also run a vulnerability scan whenever a new vulnerability database is released for the organization's scanner application. Vulnerability scanning results should be documented and discovered deficiencies should be corrected.

Organizations should also consider running more than one vulnerability scanner. As previously discussed, no scanner is able to detect all known vulnerabilities; however, using two scanners generally increases the number of vulnerabilities detected. A common practice is to use one commercial and one freeware scanner. Network-based and host-based vulnerability scanners are available for free or for a fee.

6.4.2 Penetration Testing

Penetration testing is "security testing in which evaluators attempt to circumvent the security features of a system based on their understanding of the system design and implementation".[45] The purpose of penetration testing is to exercise system protections (particularly human response to attack indications) by using common tools and techniques developed by attackers. This testing is highly recommended for complex or critical servers.

Penetration testing can be an invaluable technique to any organization's information security program. However, it is a very labor-intensive activity and requires great expertise to minimize the risk to targeted systems. At a minimum, it may slow the organization's network response time because of network mapping and vulnerability scanning. Furthermore, the possibility exists that systems may be damaged or rendered inoperable in the course of penetration testing. Although this risk is mitigated by the use of experienced penetration testers, it can never be fully eliminated.

Penetration testing does offer the following benefits:[46]

- Tests the network using the same methodologies and tools employed by attackers

- Verifies whether vulnerabilities exist

- Goes beyond surface vulnerabilities and demonstrates how these vulnerabilities can be exploited iteratively to gain greater access

- Demonstrates that vulnerabilities are not purely theoretical

- Provides the "realism" necessary to address security issues

- Allows for testing of procedures and susceptibility of the human element to social engineering.

---

[45] Definition from Committee on National Security Systems, National Information Assurance (IA) Glossary, CNSS Instruction No. 4009, June 2006
[46] Derived from John Wack et al., NIST SP 800-42, *Guideline on Network Security Testing*, February 2002, http://csrc.nist.gov/publications/PubsSPs.html

6.5 Remotely Administering a Server

Remote administration of a server should be allowed only after careful consideration of the risks. The risk of enabling remote administration varies considerably depending on the location of the server on the network. For a server that is located behind a firewall, remote administration can be implemented relatively securely from the internal network, but not without added risk. Remote administration should generally not be allowed from a host located outside the organization's network unless it is performed from an organization-controlled computer through the organization's remote access solution, such as a VPN.

If an organization determines that it is necessary to remotely administer a server, following these steps should ensure that remote administration is implemented in as secure a manner as possible:

- Use a strong authentication mechanism (e.g., public/private key pair, two-factor authentication).

- Restrict which hosts can be used to remotely administer the server.

    - Restrict by authorized users

    - Restrict by IP address (not hostname)

    - Restrict to hosts on the internal network or those using the organization's enterprise remote access solution.

- Use secure protocols that can provide encryption of both passwords and data (e.g., SSH, HTTPS); do not use less secure protocols (e.g., telnet, FTP, NFS, HTTP) unless absolutely required and tunneled over an encrypted protocol, such as SSH, SSL, or IPsec.

- Enforce the concept of least privilege on remote administration (e.g., attempt to minimize the access rights for the remote administration accounts).

- Do not allow remote administration from the Internet through the firewall unless accomplished via strong mechanisms, such as VPNs.

- Use remote administration protocols that support server authentication to prevent man-in-the-middle attacks.

- Change any default accounts or passwords for the remote administration utility or application.

Appendix A—Glossary

Selected terms used in the publication are defined below.

Availability: Ensuring that information is accessible by authorized users.

Confidentiality: Protecting information from being accessed by unauthorized parties.

Hardening: Configuring a host's operating system and applications to reduce the host's security weaknesses.

Integrity: Ensuring the authenticity of information—that information is not altered, and that the source of the information is genuine.

Least Privilege: Offering only the required functionality to each authorized user, so that no one can use functions that are not necessary.

Management Control: A security control that focuses on the management of a system or the management of risk for a system.

Network Administrator: A person responsible for the overall design, implementation, and maintenance of a network.

Operational Control: A security control that is primarily implemented and executed by people, rather than by systems.

Patch: An update to an operating system, application, or other software issued specifically to correct particular problems with the software.

Risk Assessment: The process of analyzing and interpreting risk.

Risk Management: The process of selecting and implementing controls to reduce risk to a level acceptable to the organization.

Security Administrator: A person dedicated to performing information security functions for servers and other hosts, as well as networks.

Security Control: A protection measure for a system.

Server: A host that provides one or more services for other hosts over a network as a primary function.

Server Administrator: A system architect responsible for the overall design, implementation, and maintenance of a server.

Server Software: Software that is run on a server to provide one or more services.

Service: In the context of a server, a function that a server provides for other hosts to use.

Technical Control: An automated security control employed by the system.

Upgrade: A new version of an operating system, application, or other software.

Appendix B—Acronyms and Abbreviations

Acronyms and abbreviations used in this guide are defined below.

3DES	Triple Data Encryption Standard
AES	Advanced Encryption Standard
CA	Certificate Authority
CGI	Common Gateway Interface
CIO	Chief Information Officer
CMVP	Cryptographic Module Validation Program
CPU	Central Processing Unit
DNS	Domain Name System
DoD	Department of Defense
DoS	Denial of Service
FIPS	Federal Information Processing Standard
FISMA	Federal Information Security Management Act
FOIA	Freedom of Information Act
FTP	File Transfer Protocol
HTTP	Hypertext Transfer Protocol
HTTPS	Hypertext Transfer Protocol Secure
IDPS	Intrusion Detection and Prevention System
IETF	Internet Engineering Task Force
IMAP	Internet Message Access Protocol
IP	Internet Protocol
IPsec	Internet Protocol Security
IPv4	Internet Protocol version 4
IPv6	Internet Protocol version 6
ISP	Internet Service Provider
ISSO	Information Systems Security Officer
ISSPM	Information Systems Security Program Manager
IT	Information Technology
ITL	Information Technology Laboratory
LDAP	Lightweight Directory Access Protocol
NCP	National Checklist Program
NetBIOS	Network Basic Input/Output System
NFS	Network File System
NIS	Network Information System
NIST	National Institute of Standards and Technology
NTP	Network Time Protocol
NVD	National Vulnerability Database
ODBC	Open Database Connectivity
OMB	Office of Management and Budget

OS	Operating System
PKI	Public Key Infrastructure
RAID	Redundant Array of Inexpensive Disks
RFC	Request for Comments
SHA	Secure Hash Algorithm
SHS	Secure Hash Standard
SIEM	Security Information and Event Management
SMTP	Simple Mail Transfer Protocol
SNMP	Simple Network Management Protocol
SP	Special Publication
SSH	Secure Shell
SSL	Secure Sockets Layer
TCP	Transmission Control Protocol
TLS	Transport Layer Security
URL	Uniform Resource Locator
VLAN	Virtual Local Area Network
VPN	Virtual Private Network

Appendix C—Resources

The lists below provide examples of resources that may be helpful for understanding general server security.

NIST Resource Sites

Site Name	URL
Cryptographic Module Validation Program (CMVP)	http://csrc.nist.gov/groups/STM/cmvp/index.html
National Checklist Program (NCP)	http://checklists.nist.gov/
National Vulnerability Database (NVD)	http://nvd.nist.gov/

Server Security-Specific NIST Documents

Document Title	URL
SP 800-44 Version 2, *Guidelines on Securing Public Web Servers*	http://csrc.nist.gov/publications/nistpubs/800-44-ver2/SP800-44v2.pdf
SP 800-45 Version 2, *Guidelines on Electronic Mail Security*	http://csrc.nist.gov/publications/nistpubs/800-45-version2/SP800-45v2.pdf
SP 800-81, *Secure Domain Name System (DNS) Deployment Guide*	http://csrc.nist.gov/publications/nistpubs/800-81/SP800-81.pdf

General NIST Security Documents

Document Title	URL
FIPS 140-2, *Security Requirements for Cryptographic Modules*	http://csrc.nist.gov/publications/fips/fips140-2/fips1402.pdf
FIPS 140-3 (Draft), *Security Requirements for Cryptographic Modules*	http://csrc.nist.gov/publications/PubsFIPS.html
FIPS 180-2, *Secure Hash Standard (SHS)*	http://csrc.nist.gov/publications/fips/fips180-2/fips180-2withchangenotice.pdf
FIPS 180-3 (Draft), *Secure Hash Standard (SHS)*	http://csrc.nist.gov/publications/PubsFIPS.html
FIPS 199, *Standards for Security Categorization of Federal Information and Information Systems*	http://csrc.nist.gov/publications/fips/fips199/FIPS-PUB-199-final.pdf
SP 800-14, *Generally Accepted Principles and Practices for Securing Information Technology Systems*	http://csrc.nist.gov/publications/nistpubs/800-14/800-14.pdf
SP 800-18 Revision 1, *Guide for Developing Security Plans for Federal Information Systems*	http://csrc.nist.gov/publications/nistpubs/800-18-Rev1/sp800-18-Rev1-final.pdf
SP 800-23, *Guidelines to Federal Organizations on Security Assurance and Acquisition/Use of Tested/Evaluated Products*	http://csrc.nist.gov/publications/nistpubs/800-23/sp800-23.pdf
SP 800-27 Revision A, *Engineering Principles for Information Technology Security*	http://csrc.nist.gov/publications/nistpubs/800-27A/SP800-27-RevA.pdf
SP 800-30, *Risk Management Guide for Information Technology Systems*	http://csrc.nist.gov/publications/nistpubs/800-30/sp800-30.pdf
SP 800-32, *Introduction to Public Key Technology and*	http://csrc.nist.gov/publications/nistpubs/800-32/sp800-

Document Title	URL
the Federal PKI Infrastructure	32.pdf
SP 800-34, *Contingency Planning Guide for Information Technology Systems*	http://csrc.nist.gov/publications/nistpubs/800-34/sp800-34.pdf
SP 800-37, *Guide for the Security Certification and Accreditation of Federal Information Systems*	http://csrc.nist.gov/publications/nistpubs/800-37/SP800-37-final.pdf
SP 800-40 Version 2.0, *Creating a Patch and Vulnerability Management Program*	http://csrc.nist.gov/publications/nistpubs/800-40-Ver2/SP800-40v2.pdf
SP 800-41 Revision 1 (Draft), *Guidelines on Firewalls and Firewall Policy*	http://csrc.nist.gov/publications/PubsSPs.html
SP 800-52, *Guidelines for the Selection and Use of Transport Layer Security (TLS) Implementations*	http://csrc.nist.gov/publications/nistpubs/800-52/SP800-52.pdf
SP 800-53 Revision 2, *Recommended Security Controls for Federal Information Systems*	http://csrc.nist.gov/publications/nistpubs/800-53-Rev2/sp800-53-rev2-final.pdf
SP 800-55 Revision 1, *Performance Measurement Guide for Information Security*	http://csrc.nist.gov/publications/nistpubs/800-55-Rev1/SP800-55-rev1.pdf
SP 800-60 Revision 1, Volume 1 (Draft), *Guide for Mapping Types of Information and Information Systems to Security Categories*	http://csrc.nist.gov/publications/PubsSPs.html
SP 800-61 Revision 1, *Computer Security Incident Handling Guide*	http://csrc.nist.gov/publications/nistpubs/800-61-rev1/SP800-61rev1.pdf
SP 800-63 Version 1.0.2, *Electronic Authentication Guideline*	http://csrc.nist.gov/publications/nistpubs/800-63/SP800-63V1_0_2.pdf
SP 800-63-1 (Draft), *Electronic Authentication Guideline*	http://csrc.nist.gov/publications/PubsSPs.html
SP 800-70, *Security Configuration Checklists Program for IT Products: Guidance for Checklists Users and Developers*	http://csrc.nist.gov/checklists/download_sp800-70.html
SP 800-77, *Guide to IPsec VPNs*	http://csrc.nist.gov/publications/nistpubs/800-77/sp800-77.pdf
SP 800-83, *Guide to Malware Incident Prevention and Handling*	http://csrc.nist.gov/publications/nistpubs/800-83/SP800-83.pdf
SP 800-88, *Guidelines for Media Sanitization*	http://csrc.nist.gov/publications/nistpubs/800-88/NISTSP800-88_rev1.pdf
SP 800-92, *Guide to Computer Security Log Management*	http://csrc.nist.gov/publications/nistpubs/800-92/SP800-92.pdf
SP 800-94, *Guide to Intrusion Detection and Prevention Systems (IDPS)*	http://csrc.nist.gov/publications/nistpubs/800-94/SP800-94.pdf
SP 800-100, *Information Security Handbook: A Guide for Managers*	http://csrc.nist.gov/publications/nistpubs/800-100/SP800-100-Mar07-2007.pdf
SP 800-113, *Guide to SSL VPNs*	http://csrc.nist.gov/publications/nistpubs/800-113/SP800-113.pdf
SP 800-115 (Draft), *Technical Guide to Information Security Testing*	http://csrc.nist.gov/publications/PubsSPs.html

www.ingramcontent.com/pod-product-compliance
Lightning Source LLC
Chambersburg PA
CBHW081900170526
45167CB00007B/3092